Publications of the

MINNESOTA HISTORICAL SOCIETY

RUSSELL W. FRIDLEY, *Editor and Director*

JUNE DRENNING HOLMQUIST, *Managing Editor*

AERIAL NAVIGATION COMPANY.

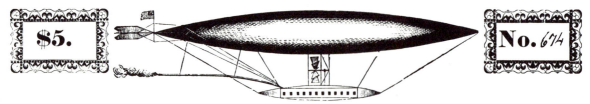

$5. No. 674

WHEREAS, I, Rufus Porter, of the city and county of Washington, and District of Columbia, have invented an apparatus denominated an AEROPORT, for the purpose of aerial navigation, and have commenced arrangements for constructing two of said aeroports—the first to be one hundred and fifty feet in length, and capable of carrying five persons, and the other to be seven hundred feet long, and capable of carrying one hundred and fifty persons, safely, at the rate of ninety miles per hour;—and whereas *William Markoe of Delafield, county of Waukesha and State of Wisconsin* has expressed a desire of obtaining an interest in said aeroports: Now this Indenture witnesseth, That for and in consideration of the sum of Five Dollars, to me in hand paid, the receipt of which is hereby acknowledged, I have assigned and transferred, and do hereby assign and transfer, to the said *Markoe* one undivided three-hundredth part of the said first aeroport that shall be constructed, and also one undivided three-thousandth part of the said second aeroport, (that is, the first that shall be constructed 700 feet in length,) the said assignee above named, or the holder hereof, to be entitled to one three-thousandth part of all benefits and emoluments that may arise or accrue from the said large aeroport for twenty years from the time the said aeroport shall have been put in operation. And I hereby covenant with the said assignee, that I will proceed forthwith and construct said two aeroports, according to my proposition and prospectus, published in the "National Intelligencer" of the 19th of March, 1852; and to keep the said large aeroport in repair for twenty years. And the master, clerks, and managers of said aeroport are hereby authorized to pay to the holders of this Indenture, on the first Monday of each month, during twenty years, one three-thousandth part of the earnings of said aeroport which shall have accrued during the month preceding. In testimony whereof, I have hereunto set my hand and affixed my seal, on this 17th day of June, 1852.

WITNESSES { B J Hobson
E. L. Porter

Rufus Porter,

A certificate of stock in Rufus Porter's Aerial Navigation Company

A YANKEE INVENTOR'S FLYING SHIP

TWO PAMPHLETS BY RUFUS PORTER · *EDITED BY RHODA R. GILMAN*

MINNESOTA HISTORICAL SOCIETY · ST. PAUL · 1969

No book is ever produced without the help of many people, and a great number have contributed to this one. The editor would like to acknowledge her debt to Mr. James Markoe, who long ago encouraged her interest in the career of his grandfather, William Markoe, and who generously gave to the Minnesota Historical Society the pamphlets that are reprinted here. Special thanks also go to Dr. Clayton F. Giese, associate professor of physics at the University of Minnesota,

A WORD OF ACKNOWLEDGMENT

Dr. A. Dale Topping, president of the Wingfoot Lighter-Than-Air Society, and Mr. Otto C. Winzen, president of Winzen Research, Inc., all of whom read the manuscript and made valuable suggestions and corrections; to Mrs. Howard Lipman, whose years of research on Porter have made her biography of him an essential source for all who follow, and who loaned her copy of the inventor's portrait; to Mr. Alan Ominsky, who designed this book and also offered much helpful counsel in its editing; and to Mr. Logan D. Gilman, the editor's husband, who more than once reached out an encouraging hand as she struggled in the deep waters of basic physics and aerodynamic theory. In the end, nevertheless, one must sink or swim alone, and all errors remain those of the editor.

Rhoda R. Gilman

CONTENTS

ILLUSTRATIONS

Rufus Porter at about the age of eighty.
PHOTOGRAPH FROM THE SMITHSONIAN INSTITUTION.

O n a succession of wintry Wednesday nights early in the year 1849, audiences in the cavernous amphitheater of New York City's Tabernacle Church at Broadway and Worth Street witnessed a curious demonstration. A toy-sized model airship, shaped like a long cigar and driven by two small propellers with clockwork motors, rose lightly from the pulpit and to the accompaniment of cheers from the watchers began a wide circle in the air. Following the tilt of its rudder, it made the round of the great chandelier that hung from the center of the dome, then returned obediently to the platform from which it was launched.[1]

Posters and handbills proclaimed the little machine the work of two men, but it was Rufus Porter, the principal inventor, who explained its construction. He also told of plans for building on the same lines a hydrogen-filled flying ship 800 feet long and capable of carrying a hundred passengers across the continent in three days. Some of the hearers were impressed, others skeptical. A few reacted like the editor of the *Philadelphia Bulletin*, who wrote after learning of the demonstrations: "It would seem as if the gullibility of human nature kept even pace

[1] *Evening Post* (New York), February 22, 1849; *Scientific American*, 4:189 (March 3, 1849).

INTRODUCTION

with the wit of knaves, and that nothing could be proposed for an exhibition too preposterous to find believers. . . . Now, a flying machine . . . can never be steered. Yet, as in the analogous instance of perpetual motion, there will be found dolts to believe in it, we suppose, to the end of time." [2]

To Americans who were more in tune with the budding scientific age the name of Rufus Porter was well known. During the previous decade he had edited and published no less than three weekly papers, two of which he had founded himself. The most popular was the *Scientific American*, started by Porter in 1845 and destined under other management to become one of the longest-lived of American periodicals. Its original subtitle proclaimed it to be "The Advocate of Industry and Enterprise, and Journal of Mechanical and Other Improvements." During Porter's two years as editor the paper lived up to this description. He tirelessly preached the gospel of universal progress through innovation, ingenuity, and initiative, and brought to public attention a flood of new ideas and inventions.[3]

In his native New England Porter was also known as an artist, for during a twenty-five-year career (off and on) as an itinerant house painter, he had left hundreds of vigorous and original murals on the walls of homes in Massachusetts, New Hampshire, and Maine. Although Porter and his clients undoubtedly regarded these only as an ingenious form of interior decoration, the murals have since established him as an important American primitive artist.

The versatile Yankee's talents ran not only to the pen and paintbrush but to the patent as well. By 1849 he had a number of inventions to his credit, including a rotary plow, an elevated railroad, a "Steam-Carriage for Common Roads," and a revolving rifle, or "bullet engine," that he had sold to Samuel Colt in 1844 for a hundred dollars. But his most ambitious project, and the one at which he persisted longest, was the airship. He claimed to have worked out the main principles of the design as early as 1820, but it was not until 1834 that he first published his plans and sought financial support. In 1841 and again in 1845 he published descriptions

[2] Quoted in *Scientific American*, 21:326 (November 20, 1869).

[3] Material here and in the following two paragraphs is drawn from Jean Lipman, *Rufus Porter: Yankee Pioneer* (New York, 1968). This ground-breaking work is the only biography of Porter and has rescued him from undeserved obscurity.

of the machine. By 1847 he had constructed a small working model which he demonstrated in New York, and it was the same model that made viewers crane their necks two years later, when Porter started a new round of promotion, hoping to take advantage of the interest in a faster and easier way to reach the California gold fields.

Among the spectators who watched in fascination and later talked earnestly with the inventor was a young Philadelphian named William Markoe. He was interested in flying. As a youth of seventeen he had become acquainted with the balloonist William Paullin and had accompanied him on ascensions over Philadelphia and Camden. In 1849, however, Markoe was studying for the Episcopal ministry and was not in a position to take to the air, either physically or financially. Nevertheless, he carried away with him a copy of one of the pamphlets here reprinted. Its sixteen pages optimistically presented Porter's plans under the title *Aerial Navigation: The Practicability of Traveling Pleasantly and Safely from New-York to California in Three Days, Fully Demonstrated.*[4]

Markoe's first parish was in Delafield, Wisconsin,

[4] See Rhoda R. Gilman, "Pioneer Aeronaut: William Markoe and His Balloon," in *Minnesota History*, 38:166–176 (December, 1963).

William Markoe in 1857.
PHOTOGRAPH FROM THE MINNESOTA HISTORICAL SOCIETY.

and while there he had ample time to study Porter's facts and figures. At last he wrote to inquire how the scheme was progressing. Porter's reply was full of confidence and enthusiasm. He had moved in 1850 from New York to Washington, D.C., where he had published the second pamphlet here reprinted, entitled *An Aerial Steamer, or Flying Ship*, of which he presumably sent Markoe a copy. He had also built and exhibited an improved model of his machine and in 1851 had organized an Aerial Navigation Company in which he was selling shares. Construction of the full-scale airship was under way, but he revealed to Markoe that "his great difficulty was want of funds." [5]

The young minister promptly sent $1,000 and accordingly, in the summer of 1852, became a major stockholder in the concern, whose original capital was only $1,500. Later Markoe persuaded his nephew to invest $1,000 and "female relatives" to put in $550 more. The only immediate benefit to stockholders was a semimonthly newsletter published under the title *Aerial Reporter*. In it Porter described the progress on his "aerial transport" or "Aeroport," and as time went by he detailed the various difficulties that caused delay. [6] Costs were invariably greater than anticipated, and the inventor appealed for more money. Still confident that the scheme would work, Markoe sent an additional sum and received a touching letter from Porter, dated August 23, 1853:

Oh! William Markoe, — All my successive, combinations of misfortunes, disappointments and adversities, even with the addition of distressing sickness in my family, have not yet moistened my eyes as did your last letter. [7]

Now, I *am* firmly determined that I will never employ a dollar of this money from you, until I can command enough to give me *assurance* of being able to complete the work, without suspension: but will hold it ready to be returned to you, if the work fails of completion.

I can not write much: you have received my Reporter No. 18 ere this; the weather has been unfavorable but we make good progress.

Yours, with sentiments undefinable

Rufus Porter

[5] Letter Books, vol. 3, p. 315, William Markoe Papers, in the Minnesota Historical Society.

[6] *Aerial Reporter*, August 14, 1852, reproduced in David P. Forsyth, *The Business Press in America, 1750–1865*, 150 (Philadelphia, 1964); Markoe Letter Books, vol. 3, p. 315.

[7] Five Porter children died in infancy during this period. The letter here quoted is in the Markoe Papers.

Despite good intentions, however, the course of things did not change. As Markoe ruefully told a friend: "Again and again I received accounts from him of the progress of the work; again and again he wrote me that everything was *almost* ready; that he was getting ready to inflate; that in about a month or a week he expected to be afloat; but invariably it would follow that some unexpected 'adverse circumstance' had knocked the whole concern on the head until the next season, when very much the same series of events would be gone through again."[8]

By the time Porter published his second pamphlet in 1850 he had reduced the proposed length of his ship from 800 to 700 feet, and the one he actually constructed was only 160 feet long and 16 feet in diameter. When it was nearly ready to test, he found that the varnish used to make the linen skin airtight had rotted the cloth. While this was being repaired a storm further damaged the ship. Never again did he come so close.[9]

In the meantime, ever concerned with publicizing his work, he had built a 22-foot steam-driven model, which he exhibited in Washington in 1853. The care with which it was decorated revealed Porter's artistic bent, for it was not only "furnished with flags and gaily painted," but had "a row of open windows on each side, and the representation of many happy looking passengers looking out at, or sitting opposite the windows."[10] Impressive though it was, it did not stimulate further investment, and Porter was forced to discontinue publication of his *Aerial Reporter* and turn to other projects.

Surprisingly, Markoe's interest in flying persisted. In 1854 he abandoned the ministry, and two years later he moved to St. Paul, Minnesota, where he invested in real estate and turned seriously to the problem of building an airship. First he wrote to Porter, urging the inventor to join him in Minnesota, where they could work together on the Aeroport. Porter's answer is not preserved, but he did not go. Markoe then got in touch with his old acquaintance Paullin and also wrote to the eminent aeronaut John Wise. On their advice he set about building a conventional balloon in order to gain experience before undertaking more hazardous ventures. After two successful flights (the first ever made in Minnesota), he again wrote to Porter.[11]

[8] Markoe Letter Books, vol. 3, p. 315.

[9] *Scientific American*, 21:326 (November 20, 1869).

[10] *Scientific American*, 21:326.

[11] Gilman, in *Minnesota History*, 38:167, 169; Markoe Letter Books, vol. 3, p. 497.

Except for the brief note quoted earlier, the inventor's lengthy answer is the only known example of Porter's personal correspondence. It is interesting for the insight it gives into the character of this ingenious nineteenth-century Yankee, who at the time of writing was sixty-five years old. His self-deception and naïveté are only too apparent, yet one cannot but respect the indomitable energy and the genuine outpouring of creativity. Had his business sense been equal to his technical insight, the world might have heard much more of Rufus Porter. The letter, dated at Washington, D.C., November 15, 1857, is printed here for the first time in its entirety.[12]

My dear Brother Marco [*sic*],

This appellation may not be agreeable to you but as it accords with the sentiments of my heart, I would not suppress it. Your two packages of extracts were very welcome and interesting, tho' they painfully excited my impatience: and the reason that I did not earlier respond, was that my hand has become nervous by long continued restraint, and that I have had five or six young men under my immediate and constant instruction, and have business writing, drawing, designing or devising at night. Your letter was received yesterday, and I thus promptly answer, tho' I shall not be able to write one fourth of the historical and other matter that I should be glad to communicate. I was never more sanguine, never more ambitious, never more assiduous in my efforts, mental and physical, in preparing the way for the introduction of my infallible project for aerial navigation. Whether it is the "prince of this world" opposes me, I know not, but I can enumerate more than one hundred untoward events and circumstances in rapid succession, and apparently out of the ordinary course of nature, and directly adverse to my progress in my preparations &c! Within the last six months I have effected nine bargains, with as many different parties, in Washington and Baltimore, most of whom made small advances of cash to bind the bargains, whereby I was to have received nearly $1500 in the aggregate, but, — will you believe it? — not even *one* of the parties, was able to raise the money to fulfil its obligation, tho' several of the parties are wealthy, and supposed they could readily command the amount; in most cases, either the parties, or those from whom they were to receive the money, were taken sick, or met with some extraordinary misfortune. The consequence has been that I have been so hard pressed that after straining my credit beyond what I had supposed possible, I have sometimes suffered for the *comforts* of life.

[12] The original is in the Markoe Papers.

I shall persevere in my efforts, and still believe that my fortune will soon turn. Among my inventions is a portable dwelling house, elegant, warm and comfortable, and which can be constructed, painted and finished for less than $200. It is composed of sections of convenient size for packing in boxes for transportation, and may be dissected taken down, or set up ready for occupancy, in two hours. I built one at Baltimore last summer, with three rooms and pantry on first floor, and two small chambers. I sold it for cash before it was finished, and afterward took it down and removed it four miles, without unhinging a door, or unshipping a window. (it has nine glass windows and five pannel [sic] doors.[)] More were wanted, and I contracted with a party to carry on the business: but they disappointed me. I am sorry I could not send you a drawing and plan of it. I am now constructing one, by the aid of a rich man, and have got it two thirds done, and there is a prospect that a hundred more will be wanted here; but, my patron has failed to pay my workmen, for want of cash, and the probability is that I shall not be able to finish it, and others will [be] afraid to take it up. They could be sent to your place for $100. I have ascertained. The following is a copy of a paper which I have prepared to present to the Heads of Departments, and perhaps the President.

An Extraordinary Statement

An American citizen who has the reputation of having done more to advance the progress of useful improvements in the United States, than any other man living, has, by many years of application and expensive experiment, succeeded in perfecting several highly important and valuable mechanical inventions, two of which are estimated by disinterested scientific men to be worth $1,000,000 each; two others are expected to save to the country more than $5,000,000 per annum besides many hundreds of human lives; two others are estimated to be worth at least $1,00[0],000 each. They have all been proved by actual and successful operation on a small scale, or in uncombined elements of full size: and have been examined and commended by the most intelligent practical scientific men, and some of them may be introduced to practical and general use for $500. Nevertheless and notwithstanding that the inventor has spent two years in unsuccessful efforts to raise the required funds for that purpose, and has offered to assign even an extravagantly liberal interest in the said inventions, yet the country and the public continue to suffer to the extent of millions of dollars per annum for want of these improvements, while not one man can be found who has $500 at command, and has at the same time, candor enough to examine, and intelligence enough to appreciate their general utility.

The inventor has applied to many of the principal ship owners of New York, and especially those of philanthropic celebrity, for aid in introducing the devices for the prevention of marine disasters; but was generally refer[r]ed to the Insurance Companies, or Board of Underwriters. The Board of Underwriters appointed a Committee to examine the subject, and the Committee reported favorably of the inventions, but that it would be inconsistent with the rules or constitution of the Board, to make any appropriation for that purpose.

The President of the Seaman's Friend Society, and of the "Association for saving the lives of shipwrecked mariners," both highly commended the inventions, but had no funds to appropriate. The inventor applied to Congress for an appropriation, but the Committees to whom the subject was referred, although they approved of the inventions were of the opinion that it was not constitutional for Congress to appropriate money to aid the introduction of new inventions.

Even the magnitude of these inventions, and of the utility thereof, operates against the inventor; the only objection opposed to them, consisting in the surmise that "if such immense improvements were bonafidely [sic] practicable, they would have been discovered before, and by some other person.["] Drawings and explanations will be presented to any person who may be disposed to examine them.

Now therefore, having become excessively impatient by long continued restraint, the inventor is inclined to offer to assign one half of all his right, title and interest in each and all of these inventions, so far as to secure to the assignee, 10,000 per cent ($100 for $1) to any gentleman or associated company who will furnish $500 for the purpose of bringing forward the said inventions.

The plan and intention of the inventor is to apply the proceeds of one of the inventions to the construction and introduction of others so that all of them may be brought into use without any additional expense to the assignee.

The Inventions are as follows:

An Engine of Defense, that will project an iron ball of 30 inches diameter, and 3600 lbs. weight to the distance of seven miles, may be constructed for $10,000, and its weight being less than 12000 lbs. it may be conveniently transported over common roads. These facts are demonstrable in theory, and an experiment of $100 expense, will establish the correctness thereof. One or two such engines would effectually protect the Chesapeak[e] Bay, or the harbor of New York.

A Self-operating Marine Pump, that may be conveniently carried on board of any sailing or steam vessel, and in case of any accidental leakage may be rigged for operation in five minutes, and will ordinarily discharge 600 gallons of water per minute, without any aid or attention from the crew. The cost of the apparatus will be only $100 each. It has been proved on a small scale, and approved by many practical and scientific men; and if generally adopted would effect a saving of $5,000,000 per annum of American property, besides hundreds of human lives. Had the "Central America" been furnished with one of these pumps, the ship would have been saved.[13]

The Sonorific Beacon is a device designed to be located upon dangerous points of the seacoasts for the purpose of giving warning to mariners of the location of danger. It is operated by the undulation of the waves or swell of the sea, and will send forth sounds far excelling those of the steam whistles of locomotives. They will require no attendance, and the cost will not exceed $300 each. A mere model, operated by an 8 inch wave, has been heard two miles. A large amount of marine property, — probably $5,000,000 per annum, — might be saved by the introduction of this invention.

[13] The "Central America" sank off Cape Hatteras on September 12, 1857. The loss was estimated at $2,400,000. See Adrian L. Lonsdale and H. R. Kaplan, *A Guide to Sunken Ships in American Waters, 51* (Arlington, Va., 1964).

An Aerial Marine Light. This invention is intended to support and display an efficient marine light, at an elevation of 500 or 1000 feet, at every point where lights are required. The expense of erecting and maintaining them will be less than one tenth part of that of common light houses. A full experiment may be made for $150.

A Simple and perfect Self-regulating and Independent Pump, that will invariably supply steam engine boilers with the precisely requisite quantity of water, without any attention from the engineer whether the engine is in motion or at rest. It has been proved by actual operation, — and would have prevented nine tenths of the steam explosions in the world [if] it had been in general use.

A Steam Farmer. (Instead of a descriptive notice, I enclose a proposition circular, which met with no encouragement here, because it was known that I was the projector of a plan for aerial navigation, which did not succeed. So the proposition is abandoned. If you know any man in your country who has the right sort of enterprise to take the whole stock and place the money in the hands of any citizen of Baltimore or Philadelphia, to be judiciously appropriated, the machine would be put in operation in early Spring, and the aeroport would follow by first of May.)

I send a copy of my first pamphlet. Of the last I

have but one copy, but intend to get a revised edition printed when I can.

Copies of Certificates

We the undersigned, citizens of Washington, D.C. have been for several years acquainted with Mr. Rufus Porter, and having regarded him as a gentleman of strict integrity as well as of scientific abilities can recommend him to the confidence of those who may be disposed to patronize his philanthropic enterprise for the prevention of marine-disasters. Washington Jan 16, 1857.

[*There follow 22 signatures.*]

I have many other certificates from scientific men in Washington and New York, in favor of my different inventions the which I need not copy. If your city editors are disposed to publish notices of my Steam Farmer and Portable Houses, I have no objection. I have not written so much at one time for two years. Please acknowledge the receipt of this: for since it has cost me so much labor I shall be anxious to know that it reaches you[.] I hope you will make no more ascensions in those dangerous ungovernable balloons. You ought to come here and help me to make nineteen fortunes, besides the aeroport.
Yours truly,
Rufus Porter

Part of Porter's difficulties at this time were no doubt caused by the panic and depression of 1857. Markoe also had felt the effects. Land values in Minnesota collapsed overnight and ready cash was almost nonexistent. During the winter and spring of 1857-58 he reconditioned and enlarged his balloon in preparation for further flights, but these were never made. While he was preparing to launch on a morning in early June, 1858, a strong wind came up, and the nearly inflated balloon, strained beyond the strength of its material, ripped from top to bottom. This ended Markoe's aerial experiments "for many a long day," as he wrote to Porter nearly a year later.[14] Investing in a brickyard and other business ventures, he lived out a long and quiet life as a leading citizen of St. Paul.

By the mid 1800s Markoe and Porter were far from alone in their dreams of controlled human flight. Hardly had men soared aloft beneath the first balloons in 1783 than they began to devise schemes for propelling and guiding the free-floating spheres. Literally hundreds of plans were proposed, most of them totally impractical, but slowly, by costly trial

[14] Markoe Letter Books, vol. 4, p. 54.

and by errors that often ended in tragedy, men groped their way toward an understanding of aerodynamic principles. In the meantime advances in other fields were steadily making their efforts more effective. The harnessing of steam and electricity and later the perfecting of the internal combustion engine eventually provided a motive power sufficient for the task, while the development of lighter and stronger materials, such as aluminum, and the improvement of techniques for producing hydrogen and coal gas made buoyancy less of a problem.[15]

The first ideas were keyed to the technology of the eighteenth century. Sails and oars appeared in many designs and were actually carried on a few flights, where they proved hopelessly ineffective. Even the harnessing of birds was suggested from time to time. Several ingenious tinkerers sought to combine the principles of the balloon and the glider to achieve forward motion, while the more thoughtful inventors quickly perceived the disadvantage of

[15] There are numerous general works on the history of aeronautics. See, for example, M. J. B. Davy, *Interpretive History of Flight: A Survey of the History and Development of Aeronautics* (London, 1948); L. T. C. Rolt, *The Aeronauts: A History of Ballooning 1783–1903* (New York, 1966).

the balloon's globular shape and proposed an elongated gas bag to reduce air resistance. The most advanced early design was devised before 1785 by Jean Baptiste Marie Meusnier, an engineering officer of the French army. He suggested an elliptical balloon driven by a screw propeller and also outlined a means for preserving the elongated shape under varying gas pressure. This invention, known as the ballonet, remained basic to all streamlined airships except those using a rigid framework.

Human brawn was the only motive force available to Meusnier, and it continued to be the power source in the vast majority of airship designs until well past the middle of the nineteenth century. If Porter was right in claiming that he developed the main principles of his invention as early as 1820, he was without question far ahead of his time. No one else had then suggested a steam-driven airship.

Even by 1834, when he published his plans in the *Mechanics' Magazine*, Porter was well in advance of other designers. The major aeronautical sensation of that year occurred in France where the Comte de Lennox promoted a London-Paris airline to be operated with a 130-foot dirigible christened the "Eagle." The ship was to be propelled by eight enormous flapping paddles manned by a large crew. At its first

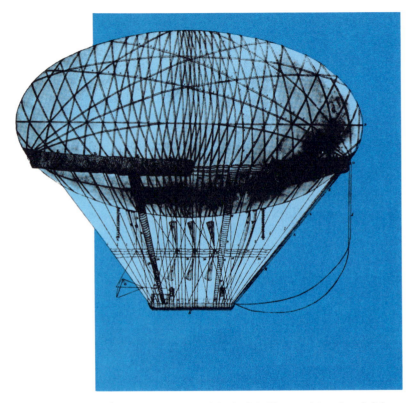

Meusnier's design for an elliptical balloon with a hand-driven screw propeller, first proposed in the early 1780s.

exhibition the machine failed to get off the ground and was torn to pieces by the disappointed spectators. A second model constructed in London the following year was no more successful. Compared with the "Eagle," Porter's slim design with its rigid, streamlined framework, enclosed gondola, and steam-driven propeller was indeed sophisticated.[16]

By the late 1840s, when Porter was exhibiting his first operating model in New York, steam transportation had come into its own, and a number of serious inventors were seeking to apply to aerial navigation the new motive power that was working marvels on sea and land. Another American, John H. Pennington, showed drawings of a "steam balloon" (appropriately called the "New Era") which was to be driven by a paddle wheel and guided with a large rudder. Unconcernedly, Pennington ran the smokestack from his burner directly through the hydrogen-filled gas bag and funneled it out the top.[17]

[16] Rolt, *The Aeronauts,* 207. Porter's first version of the aerial transport, described and illustrated in *Mechanics' Magazine,* 4:273–275 (November 8, 1834), differed in a number of details from his 1849 plan. See picture, p. 15.

[17] Pennington's earlier designs are described in Jeremiah Milbank, Jr., *The First Century of Flight in America,* 78 (Princeton, N.J., 1943). His steam balloon is shown in a broadside dated 1845 which is reproduced on p. 13.

In 1844 and again in 1850 miniature power-driven craft were demonstrated in Paris, and it was over the French capital on September 24, 1852 — while Porter still struggled to build his Aeroport in Washington — that Henri Giffard made the first successful journey in a power-driven airship. Using an elongated balloon pointed at each end and a three-horsepower steam engine attached to a car some forty feet below the inflammable gas bag, Giffard traveled seventeen miles and achieved a speed of about six miles an hour.[18]

Although many aerial monstrosities were still to be proposed, and a few were actually built, the mainstream of dirigible development had been established, and Porter's design was well within it. The pointed cylindrical shape was modified in many ways, but it remained the basic general form of most successful airships. Powered flight also had come to stay, although the heavy steam engine was replaced by the electric motor in experiments made by Gaston and Albert Tissandier in 1883 and by Charles Renard and Arthur Krebs in 1884. An early form of internal combustion engine was used on a balloon in 1872, but the small, high-speed gasoline engine was

[18] Rolt, *The Aeronauts*, 209.

PENNINGTON'S Steam — NEWLY INVENTED Balloon.

NEW ERA.

COURTESY OF KENNETH M. NEWMAN,
THE OLD PRINT SHOP, NEW YORK CITY.

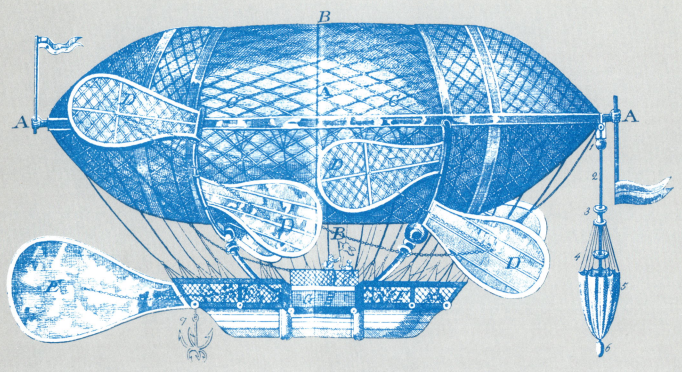

An artist's conception of the "Eagle," built in 1834,
the year Porter first publicized his plan.

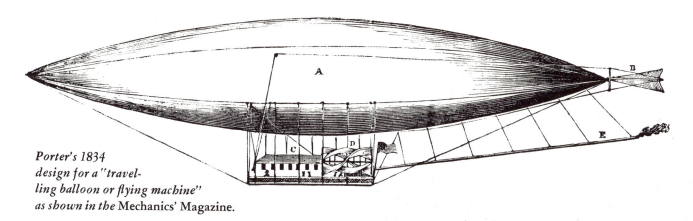

*Porter's 1834
design for a "travel-
ling balloon or flying machine"
as shown in the* Mechanics' Magazine.

not developed until the late 1880s by Gottfried Daimler in Germany. It was first applied to dirigibles in the 1890s by Karl Woelfert and David Schwartz. The close of the century saw the true era of aerial navigation begin with the use of light and powerful gasoline engines by Alberto Santos-Dumont in France and by Count Ferdinand von Zeppelin in Germany. No one then foresaw that the entire principle of buoyant or lighter-than-air flight

[19] *Mechanics' Magazine*, 4:275. Jonathan Hulls, a Gloucestershire clockmaker, published his scheme for applying steam power to a boat in 1737. See Robert Macfarlane, *History of Propellers and Steam Navigation*, 13–16 (New York, 1851).

would be superseded in little more than a generation by the rapid advances to be made in mechanical flight or aviation.

After describing his design in 1834, Porter wrote prophetically: "Such is my plan for flying; and as the immortal Fulton ventured to build a steamboat seventy years after Jonathan Hulls had published his plan for the same, I shall indulge the hope that some enterprising person will within another seventy years build and put in successful operation a manageable balloon."[19] That this prediction was all too accurate would probably have disturbed Porter less than the fact that his own ideas made little impres-

The first successful power-driven airship, piloted by the French inventor and engineer Henri Giffard in 1852.

sion on the scientific community and had long been forgotten by the time later inventors designed the first successful dirigibles.

One of the reasons for this neglect was shrewdly suggested by John Wise, who wrote in 1850: "Had these projectors [*R. Porter and Company*] gone on from their miniature model, to the erection of one capable of carrying one or two persons, in order to prove its practicability on a larger scale, there might have been reason to believe that they harbored an idea of its general usefulness. But when the project embraced at once so magnificent a scheme, as that contemplated in the swooping strides towards the modern *El Dorado*, with a cargo of a hundred gold hunters, it seemed too much for sober-minded people. And . . . it brought upon itself philosophical criticism and scientific condemnation, and with that, a good share of opposition to the hopes and expectations of aerial navigation in any shape."[20]

Geography also worked against Porter. From 1783 until the early twentieth century France was the acknowledged leader of the world in aeronauti-

[20] John Wise, *A System of Aeronautics, Comprehending Its Earliest Investigations, and Modern Practice and Art*, 101 (Philadelphia, 1850).

cal research and experimentation. International scientific communication was limited at best in the nineteenth century, and Porter was not the only American airship inventor to be ignored and forgotten. Pennington suffered the same fate, as did Dr. Solomon Andrews with his "Aereon" and Frederick Marriott, whose 37-foot "Avitor," a steam-powered model, flew successfully in California in 1869. There were others of whom history has preserved even fainter traces.[21]

In 1966 Markoe's papers were presented to the Minnesota Historical Society by a grandson, Mr. James Markoe. Among them are the two Porter letters quoted above, a stock certificate of the Aerial Navigation Company, a single copy (Volume I, Number 8) of the *Aerial Reporter*, a printed prospectus for shares in the development of the "steam

farmer," and the two pamphlets on the Aeroport. Some of these materials are unique and all are extremely rare.

The items of widest general interest are the two pamphlets here reprinted. *Aerial Navigation* (New York, 1849) was reissued in a small edition in 1935 (San Francisco, Lawton R. Kennedy) with an introduction by Admiral Herbert V. Wiley, then commander of the naval airship "U.S.S. Macon." Of the original edition only two other copies are known: one is in the library of Yale University, and the other is owned by Harvard University. The Minnesota Historical Society has the only known copy of *An Aerial Steamer, or Flying Ship* (Washington, D.C., 1850). Together, the two little booklets contain the core of Porter's plan for building an airship, along with his glowing journalist's vision of the future of aerial navigation.

Of the two pamphlets, the 1849 one is the longer and more interesting. The original measures 9½ by 6 inches and numbers sixteen pages. Its front cover announces the title as *Aerial Navigation: The Practicability of Traveling Pleasantly and Safely from New-York to California in Three Days, Fully Demonstrated: With a Full Description of a Perfect Aerial Locomotive, with Estimates of Capacity,*

[21] On Andrews and Marriott see Milbank, *First Century of Flight in America*, 82–88, 90–93; Solomon Andrews, *The Art of Flying* (New York, 1865), and *The Aereon* (New York, 1866); Richard A. Hernandez, "Frederick Marriott: A 'Forty-Niner Banker and Editor Who Took a 'Flier' in Pioneering American Aviation," in *Journal of the West*, 2:401 (October, 1963); T. H. Watkins, "The Revoloidal Spindle and the Wondrous Avitor," in *American West*, February, 1967, p. 24.

Speed, and Cost of Construction. The author is identified as "Original Editor of the New-York Mechanic, Scientific American and Scientific Mechanic." The place of publication is "New-York" and the publisher is identified as H. Smith of "128 Fulton-Street, Sun Buildings; room 40"—the same address given on the back cover for R. Porter & Company. The pamphlet was printed by John Hall of 222 Water Street. Inside, a separate title page repeats this information exactly, except that the address of the publisher is omitted.

The back cover carries a drawing of the Aeroport, labeled only "BEST ROUTE TO CALIFORNIA." The picture does not represent the true scale of the design, for the dimensions of both car and aerostat are greatly distorted. Also the car, or "saloon" as Porter called it, is shown nearly as long as the aerostat, whereas by the inventor's figures it would have been only a little more than one quarter the length. Beneath this illustration is the following statement:

R. PORTER & CO., (office, room No. 40 in the Sun Buildings,—entrance 128 Fulton-street, New-York,) are making active progress in the construction of an Aerial Transport, for the express purpose of carrying passengers between New York and California. This transport will have a capacity to carry from 50 to 100 passengers, at a speed of 60 to 100 miles per hour. It is expected to put this machine in operation about the 1st of April, 1849. It is proposed to carry a limited number of passengers — not exceeding 300 — for $50, including board, and the transport is expected to make a trip to the gold region and back in seven days. The price of passage to California is fixed at $200, with the exception above mentioned. Upwards of 200 passage tickets at $50 each have been engaged prior to Feb. 15. Books open for subscribers as above.

The direct appeal for subscriptions is not repeated within. Instead Porter devotes the text of his pamphlet to a discussion of the physical principles of aerial navigation aimed at the informed "mechanic" or layman and to a detailed description of his invention, including estimates of weight and cost for its various parts. On the closing page he envisions for the reader the delights of soaring above the earth in perfect comfort and security. With optimism characteristic of his times, he foresaw nothing but benefits to mankind from the approaching age of air travel.

The second pamphlet, *An Aerial Steamer, or Flying Ship*, is a pocket-sized prospectus measuring 6⅞ by 4½ inches and containing only twelve pages. Beneath the title on the front cover is a drawing of the Aeroport, modified somewhat from the 1849 version. The scale and proportion, though a little closer to reality, are still not accurate. Design changes have apparently been made in the arrangement of the supports and in the shape and position of the propellers. No author is indicated, but Rufus Porter's name appears prominently as the inventor, and he is identified as in the 1849 pamphlet. Publication information includes only "W. Greer, Printer, Washington, D.C., 1850." This booklet has no separate title page.

The text is written in the third person, but the style clearly indicates Porter's authorship. In the first two and a half pages he briefly describes the machine; the next section, entitled, "Speed or Velocity," is a condensed version of his earlier discussion of aeronautical principles; under the heading "Management" he considers some of the practical details of operation; and in a closing section on "Safety" he undertakes to answer some of the objections made by critics of the plan. California is not mentioned. A note of frustration is evident in the final paragraph, where Porter directs bitter words at "capitalists" who have refused to back his scheme.

The last page includes five short extracts from New York and Boston newspapers concerning the successful demonstration of his model. There is no back cover.

Both pamphlets are cheaply printed on inexpensive paper. Only obvious typographical errors have been corrected in the two reprints below. Inaccuracies of spelling or punctuation and oddities of language have been preserved. No attempt has been made to annotate all Porter's errors in mathematics and logic nor to underscore the overoptimism of most of his assumptions. The reader must keep in mind that Porter was proposing what he thought were workable answers in a situation where experimentation and research had not yet fully established the nature of the questions.

His aerial transport would never have performed as he envisioned it. With the materials and technology available to him the problems of weight, power, and structural stress were far too great. But as Admiral Wiley pointed out in his introduction to the 1935 edition of *Aerial Navigation*, Porter's design had many sound and farsighted features. His "float" or aerostat, for example, was based on the principle of a rigid framework later employed by Zeppelin. Like the Zeppelin plan, also, it was to be separated into independent airtight compartments, one or two of which might be damaged and still leave the ship afloat. By a long exhaust pipe, Porter sought to insure that flying cinders from the burner would be carried well to the rear of the ship. His rudder had both vertical and horizontal planes, and he recognized the necessity of trimming the craft. Finally, his analysis of aerodynamic principles, while faulty in a number of ways, was remarkably keen for the time. It is especially impressive in a man who possessed no academic credentials and had received no formal schooling beyond the age of twelve. Largely on the evidence in the two pamphlets re-

printed here, a leading historian of early American flight has concluded that "Rufus Porter, as the designer of one of the first important patents and the previewer of modern airship construction, has claim to an important niche in the hall of American aeronautical fame." [22]

[22] Milbank, *First Century of Flight in America*, 78. An anonymous writer in the magazine *Aviation*, 8:145 (March 15, 1920) suggested: "Now that the United States Navy has decided to build up a fleet of large rigid airships, it would seem the fitting thing to give these important units the names of American airship pioneers. The memory of Rufus Porter undoubtedly deserves to be thus honored among the first." For a variety of reasons the Navy paid no heed.

The front cover of Porter's first pamphlet (at right) and illustrated back cover (over).

AERIAL NAVIGATION:

THE PRACTICABILITY OF TRAVELING PLEASANTLY AND SAFELY FROM

NEW-YORK TO CALIFORNIA

IN THREE DAYS,

FULLY DEMONSTRATED:

WITH A FULL DESCRIPTION OF A PERFECT AERIAL LOCOMOTIVE,
WITH ESTIMATES OF CAPACITY, SPEED, AND
COST OF CONSTRUCTION.

By RUFUS PORTER,

ORIGINAL EDITOR OF THE NEW-YORK MECHANIC, SCIENTIFIC
AMERICAN AND SCIENTIFIC MECHANIC.

NEW-YORK :
PUBLISHED BY H. SMITH.
128 *Fulton-Street, Sun Buildings ; room* 40.
JOHN HALL, PRINTER, 222 WATER-STREET.
1849.

BEST ROUTE TO CALIFORNIA.

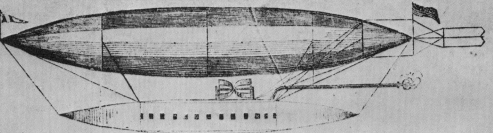

R. PORTER & CO., (office, room No. 40 in the Sun Buildings,—entrance 128 Fulton-street, New-York,) are making active progress in the construction of an Aerial Transport, for the express purpose of carrying passengers between NewYork and California. This transport will have a capacity to carry from 50 to 100 passengers, at a speed of 60 to 100 miles per hour. It is expected to put this machine in operation about the 1st of April, 1849. It is proposed to carry a limited number of passengers—not exceeding 300—for $50, including board, and the transport is expected to make a trip to the gold region and back in seven days. The price of passage to California is fixed at $200, with the exception above mentioned. Upwards of 200 passage tickets at $50 each have been engaged prior to Feb. 15. Books open for subscribers as above.

It has been the expressed opinion of the wisest and most philosophic men of at least two centuries past, that Aerial Navigation was practicable, and would eventually come into practical use. But its introduction has been greatly retarded by the many futile and unscientific pretensions made by visionary persons who had neglected to acquaint themselves with the general and established principles of the true natural (or Newtonian) philosophy. The vague and unreasonable assumption of novices, has had the deleterious effect to destroy or weaken the confidence of wealthy business men in the practicability of traveling with safety through the air. One of these vagaries, which was first introduced by a Mr. Roberts in 1784, and recently revived by a man in New Hampshire, consisted in the foolish idea of directing the motion of a common balloon by means of adjustable sails;[1] the projectors ignorantly overlooking the fact, that no sail could be

[1] By "Mr. Roberts" Porter may have meant one of the two French aerial pioneers, Anne-Jean and Marie-Noel Robert. These brothers, who assisted the French scientist Jacques A. C. Charles in developing the hydrogen balloon in 1783, made a number of experiments, including the use of oars and of elongated balloons, but they are not known to have been associated with an attempt to navigate by sails alone. The man in New Hampshire has not been identified.

AERIAL NAVIGATION

filled or affected by the wind, while the entire apparatus or vehicle, to which the sails are connected, floats passively along with the aerial current. Several other plans have been projected (and as often exploded) for elevating and propelling a machine on the principle of the flight of birds, by the force of mechanical power and without the aid of buoyancy. But the authors of all these projects have discovered, what they should have known before they attempted an experiment, that there is no power known — not even that of gunpowder — that is capable of sustaining the weight of its own requisite apparatus, by means of either wings or spiral fan-wheels, for any length of time.

Another plan has been proposed, and that by practical balloonists, who should have known better, for propelling common balloons by steam power. But the projectors of this plan must have been ignorant of the laws of atmospheric resistance; to overcome which would require more than 1,000 horse-powers to a balloon that would carry twenty passengers at the rate of sixty miles an hour; and they must also have overlooked the fact, that with such a velocity, the atmospheric resistance would be sufficient to destroy or rend any material used in ordinary balloons. But the silliest plan that we have seen pro-

posed, was that of Muzzio Muzzi the Italian who raised a considerable excitement on the subject in this (New York) city in 1845, and who, we are grieved to say, managed to obtain the approbation of several gentlemen of high standing and reputation as the first scientific men of New York.[2] We had the pleasure, or rather the mortification, to witness an exhibition of the project of the popular foreigner (and with a fuller house than any native American could draw on a similar occasion), and immediately published in the first number of the "Scientific American" [*August 28, 1845*], an expose which proved a *killer* to the popular humbug. The following is a copy: —

[2] Muzio Muzzi patented his device in 1844 and demonstrated a model the following year in the chapel of New York University. See Milbank, *First Century of Flight in America*, 79–81. Porter's diagram was apparently simplified in order to illustrate the principle on which the device operated.

[3] This reference is, of course, to Porter's own design, which was published in the *Mechanics' Magazine* in 1834 and in the *New York Mechanic* in 1841.

SIGNOR MUZZI'S TRAVELLING BALLOON

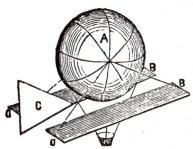

"This cut sufficiently represents the machine which consists of a balloon or ball (A), made of oiled silk or paper, and filled with hydrogen gas. To this balloon are attached two inclined planes (BB) which are also constructed of light materials and secured in their position by cords. In addition, there is a triangular vane, tale or rudder (C) by which the machine is steered on the principle of a helm. The plan, or mode of operating the machine, is to supply it with a sufficient quantity of gas to cause it to ascend, while the inclined planes, encountering some degree of atmospheric resistance, naturally shoot off in an oblique direction, drawing the balloon with them. Then, when the machine has ascended to a sufficient height, a part of the gas is to be let off or compressed, so as to cause the balloon to descend, and by a simple contrivance, the position of the two planes is reversed, the depressed ends being brought to the front, they give the balloon an oblique direction in its descent. Thus, by ascending a mile and again descending, a mile of horizontal distance is gained; and if the atmosphere be entirely calm, a mile may be travelled about as quick as a lame man would walk the same distance. But if there be the least breeze of head wind, the game is up. And by what means the balloon is to be made to again ascend, without a fresh supply of gas, the inventor has not informed us — perhaps he does not exactly know.

Such, gentle reader, is the invention which has been lauded by our first men and biggest editors, and of which an awkward model has received "rounds of applause" from a "select and fashionable audience" (who paid fifty cents each to witness the wonder,) as the nearest approach to successful aerial navigation that has ever been thought of, notwithstanding that ten years ago, in a popular public journal of this city, — and again four years ago, in another city paper, — a plan was presented to them, with ample illustrations, explanations and demonstrations of an aerial apparatus, on perfectly rational and established principles, that will evidently navigate the atmosphere at a speed of one hundred miles per hour, with safety, and perfectly at command; [3] being in the form of an *eliptic spindle*, with a buoyancy of several tons, and driven forward by the power of steam, applied to revolving, spiral fan-wheels. Why then, it may be asked, has this *new plan* produced so much excitement, amongst the very people who appeared totally indifferent to the *rational* plan? The answer is, simply, that the scientific plan was introduced by an American, while the new apparatus was invented by an *Italian* gentleman — the audience knowing but little of the merits of either.

With regard to the inventor, — Signor Muzzi, — he appears to be an unassuming gentleman, desirous of procuring assistance to put his invention in successful operation on a large scale. In this we may well sympathize with him, and heartily wish him all possible success; but we should be glad to have our citizens of scientific pretensions, become better informed in the principles of natural philosophy, than they have manifested on this occasion."

It is a fact, the most astonishing and unaccountable fact that is known to exist, that the masses of otherwise intelligent men, persist in downright ignorance of even the main and general principles of natural philosophy; but thus it is, and hence arises the grand difficulty which inventors have to encounter in introducing the most useful and important inventions, while the most gross and ridiculous humbugs are lauded and patronized, and the explosions thereof are muffled and concealed.

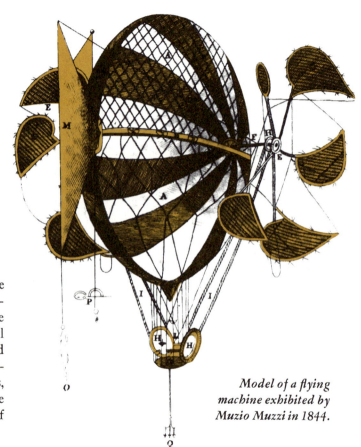

Model of a flying machine exhibited by Muzio Muzzi in 1844.

To establish the practicability of aerial locomotion, nothing more is required than the combination of three general and well-established principles: first, that a vessel containing hydrogen gas is buoyant in atmospheric air; second, that a revoloidal spindle of any size may be propelled through the air at a rapid rate, without any considerable atmospheric resistance; and third, that a spiral fan-wheel or screw propeller will effect a propulsive power by action on atmospheric air.

It is a very easy thing for wise men, or even reputed scientific men, to shake their heads with the exclamation — "moonshine!" but it is a notorious fact, that the scientific men of New York and of the world have been repeatedly challenged to produce any argument or reason against the feasibility of the plan herein proposed and described. But, hitherto, no person has attempted a scientific refutation, though many are ready enough to denounce this plan as impracticable, because it has not been done before.

It has been generally well known that hydrogen gas, being much lighter, has a buoyant power in atmospheric air; and that the figure known geometrically as the *revoloidal spindle*, will encounter less resistance in passing through the air than either a ball or a cylinder; but it has not been known to what extent, or in what proportion this difference exists.[4] It is demonstrable however, that a revoloidal spindle, whose length is equal to sixteen times its diameter, will encounter, in passing through the air, less than 1-3000th part of the atmospheric resistance that would be encountered by a cylinder of equal diameter, and running with equal velocity. With regard to the atmospheric resistance encountered by a plain surface passing rapidly through the air, different authors disagree, but we admit it to be equal to 32 lbs per square foot of surface moving at the rate of 100 miles per hour, or 146 feet per second.[5] Of course, the resistance encountered by the end of a cylinder 50 feet in diameter, and moving with that

[4] A spindle is defined by the *Century Dictionary and Cyclopedia* (1889) as "a solid generated by the revolution of the arc of a curve about its chord. The spindle is denominated circular, elliptic, hyperbolic, parabolic, etc. according to the figure of its generating curve." The term "revoloidal" does not seem to have been commonly used even in the mid-nineteenth century, though it is doubtful that Porter coined it. As he indicates above, in the article quoted from the *Scientific American*, he had in mind an elliptic spindle.

[5] This figure, which may have been established by measurement, is reasonably close to the presently accepted theoretical figure of 25 pounds per square foot, assuming an infinite plane. Porter's assertion in the following lines that resistance varies as the square of the velocity is correct for low velocities such as he dealt with.

velocity, would be 62,000 lbs. But we shall show that the resistance encountered by a revoloidal spindle of equal diameter and moving with equal velocity, is less than 20 lbs. It is a well-known law of nature, that the resistance of a fluid is as the square of the velocity of the moving body passing through it; and the resistance is increased or diminished as the square of the increase or diminution of the velocity. Therefore, if the velocity is reduced from 146 to 73 feet per second, the resistance is reduced from 32 to 8 lbs per square foot. If the velocity is 37 feet, the resistance is only 2 lbs. By the same rule, if the velocity is 9 feet, the resistance is only .125; and if the velocity is 4.5 feet, the resistance is only .031 of 1 lb per square foot. By the motion of a revoloidal spindle through the atmosphere, the air is removed, not in the direction of the motion of the spindle, but in a direction at right angles with the surface thereof. And, it may be observed, by examining the surface of a spindle of the above-mentioned proportions, that the average velocity with which the air is put in motion, by the passage of the spindle, is only about 1-30th of the velocity of the spindle in its course; so that, if the spindle is moving at the rate of 100 miles per hour, the motion of the removed air is only about 5 feet per second, and its

resistance is consequently less than one thirtieth of a pound per square foot. And this resistance, being not counter to the motion of the spindle, but at right angles to the surface thereof; the entire resistance to the motion of the spindle is only equal to 1-30th of a pound per square foot of the area of the spindle, which being 1900 feet, the entire resistance, even by this rule, would be but 66 lbs.[6] But even this resistance is greatly reduced by the elasticity of the atmosphere, and by the excessive pressure of the atmosphere in proportion to the weight or gravity of the air. The weight of air is but little more than one ounce per cubic foot, while the atmospheric pressure is upwards of 2000 lbs upon every square foot of surface. This circumstance, in connexion with the well known elasticity of the air, renders it evident that the atmospheric pressure upon the rear half of the spindle is very nearly equal to that on the forward half — the difference is inappreciable. Was the body of air which is removed by the spindle sud-

[6] Porter's argument concerning the angle of motion of displaced air shows considerable insight. He did not, however, allow for the viscosity of air. A small layer of air (boundary layer) clings to the surface of the moving object and moves with it, creating added resistance as it shears away from the adjoining layers.

denly encountered thereby, and put in motion at the rate of five feet per second (as would be the case if encountered by a wedge shaped figure), and as suddenly returned to its former position, the resistance would be more considerable; but the spindle being pointed, a small portion of surface first produces a very slight motion in the surrounding air, which motion is gradually increased till its velocity reaches 5 feet per second; and is then brought to rest, and as gradually returned to its former position: and it yet remains doubtful whether any difference could be detected between the atmospheric pressure on the forward part of the spindle and that on the rearward part.[7] Was air non-elastic, like water, so that a large body of it was required to be removed, or did it depend on its own gravity to return to its original position when the swelled centre of the spindle had passed, the case would be different. But it is obvious that, by the elasticity of the air and the atmospheric pressure combined, the air will continue its pressure against all parts of the surface of the spindle equally, or nearly so; and, conse-

quently, the actual resistance to the forward motion of the spindle must be trivial, probably not exceeding 10 lbs with a velocity of 100 miles per hour.

A revoloidal spindle 800 feet long, and 50 feet in diameter, contains 838,000 cubic feet, and being inflated with hydrogen gas, the weight of which is 36 grs. per cubic foot, while that of atmospheric air is 527 grains, its buoyant power in air would be 56,000 lbs. Measures being now in progress for constructing such a spindle, or aerial float, we shall proceed to describe it.

Twenty-four spruce rods are to be employed, each rod being an inch and a half in diameter and 800 feet long. These rods are united at each end, and the central parts are bent outward, so as to form the skeleton or frame work of a spindle of 50 feet in diameter, and this frame is covered with cloth coated with gum elastic (India rubber). The rods are six feet apart at the centres, and the cloth is attached to each. A saloon, 180 feet long and 10 feet square at the centre, tapering to a point at each end, is suspended by flattened steel wires about 60 feet below the float. This saloon is made of painted cloth, supported by a very light frame work, and about 80 feet of the central part is furnished with windows, and a floor of thin boards sustained by

---

[7] In this argument Porter erroneously assumes the complete elasticity of air. There would, in fact, be greater pressure on the forward part.

four rows of vertical wires extending upward to the float. The saloon is also furnished with seats, which may be readily transformed to beds for those who may have occasion to sleep on board. In the centre of the saloon is an apartment 6 feet by 12, in which are adjusted six light tubular boilers of two horse-powers each, and two steam engines, the power of which is applied to two fan wheels or propellers mounted between the float and the saloon. The smoke from the engine fires is conducted 100 feet or more to the rear by a horizontal pipe. The boilers and engines are supported by strips of steel plate the tops of which are attached to the rods of the float at several different points. Near the engine room is an aperture four feet wide and eight feet long through the floor of the saloon; and this aperture is closed by an elevator, consisting of a platform furnished with seats and railings, and suspended by ropes attached to its four corners. These ropes meet and are united in one about ten feet above the elevator, and this one rope passes over a pulley, and thence to a windlass shaft furnished with cranks and ratchets, and which may be connected to one of the steam engines.[8] One of the ratchets serves as an escapement wheel and has a balance verge, so adjusted that the elevator can never descend rapidly; and the elevator is furnished with a small cord, one end of which is attached to the balance verge, so that any person descending by the elevator can instantly stop or check its descent whenever occasion requires. The elevator is drawn up either by the cranks or by steam power.

To the rear end of the float is connected, by a ball and socket or universal joint, a rudder 20 feet long and having four leaves, two of them horizontal and two vertical, each leaf being five feet wide, and consisting of thin boards or sheets of wood, projecting obliquely from a centre bar, and each board tapering from a quarter to a sixteenth of an inch in thickness. From the outward edge of each of the four leaves, a cord extends forward, passing over a pulley, and thence down to the saloon; so that the helmsman can change the position of the rudder, either vertically or horizontally, as occasion may require. It will be readily understood that the machine (which, for want of a better name, is called

---

[8] This arrangement, terminating in a single rope and pulley, would allow uncontrolled spinning of the elevator about its vertical axis when being raised or lowered. Apparently Porter recognized the problem, for in his second pamphlet (p. 42) the ropes from the four corners pass over four separate pulleys.

An aerial monstrosity proposed by Ernest Pétin, a French contemporary of Porter, who lectured on aeronautics in New York's Tabernacle Church in 1852.

an AERIAL LOCOMOTIVE), may be made to ascend or descend, as well as to change its horizontal direction, by means of this rudder.

To each of the twenty-four rods within the float is attached a small cord, and the 24 cords meet at the centre of the float, and passing over twenty-four pulleys, unite in one rope, which after extending a few feet horizontally, passes over another pulley downward, and is connected to a small iron rod, which passes down through a stuffing box in the bottom of the float, and is connected to another rope which extends down to a crank windlass within the saloon; so that by turning the windlass, the entire series of rods are drawn centreward, and the volume of the float may be compressed, and its buoyancy sufficiently reduced to cause it to descend. A compression of a single inch on all sides is sufficient to reduce the buoyancy 36 lbs; and the strength of a man applied one minute to the crank is sufficient to reduce the buoyancy 200 lbs. These contracting lines may be arranged at several different points in the length of the float, and managed by two vertical contracting rods and two windlass cranks; so that either the forward or rearward part of the float may be compressed occasionally, by which the opposite end will become distended. This arrangement will sometimes be useful in keeping the float in horizontal trim.[9]

The two propelling wheels are each 20 feet in diameter, having eight arms, and to each is attached an oblique sail seven feet wide at the outward end and eight feet long: the whole presenting about 700 square feet of surface. These wheels will make 200 revolutions per minute, in order to propel the locomotive 100 miles per hour.

It has been before stated that the buoyant power of the float is 56,000 lbs. We shall now proceed to a careful estimate of the quantity and weight of all the materials employed in the construction of the apparatus.

	Lbs.
20,000 feet of spruce rods, equal to 2000 feet board measure, estimated at 2 lbs per foot,	4000
8,000 yards of vulcanized cloth, at ½ lb per yard	4000
800 feet of ½ inch boards for floor of saloon,	800
300 yards painted cloth for saloon, ...	150
12,000 feet of cast steel wire	300
Seats and furniture	500
Six boilers and two engines	2000
Two propelling wheels	500
Fuel and water for 12 hours	1000
Rudder and ropes	450
Sundries, overlooked in the above estimate . .	300

Total weight, ... 14,000

Leaving a balance of buoyancy of 42,000 lbs, sufficient for 200 passengers and their baggage.

To show the advantage of a machine of the foregoing dimensions over one of a smaller size, we sub-

[9] Here Porter acknowledged a problem that was ignored by most of his contemporaries, although his device for solving it was clumsy and probably unworkable. He was apparently unaware that a better solution for keeping an elongated balloon in trim had been offered in 1789. An air bag or ballonet at each end could be inflated or deflated to vary the buoyancy. See Davy, *Interpretive History of Flight*, 43.

join an estimate of one of half the diameter and one-fourth of the length of the above-described.

Length, 200 feet; diameter, 25 feet; contents 52,370 cubic feet; buoyancy, 3,500 lbs.

Weight of 800 yards of cloth	400
2,400 feet of rods	400
Cloth for saloon (50 long, 6 diameter) 74 yards	37
Floor of saloon, 150 feet of thin boards	150
Suspending wires 3,000 feet	63
Propelling wheels	150
Rudder, ropes, and belts	60
Total weight without an engine,	1,260

Leaving a balance of buoyancy of 2,240 lbs.

A four-horse power engine	700
Water and fuel	400
Total weight	2,360

[10] This statement is untrue, but Porter's insistence on the greater efficiency of a large airship had some justification. In 1837 the British scientist Sir George Cayley pointed out that the volume of an ordinary balloon increases more rapidly than its surface, and hence the lifting power of a large balloon is greater in proportion to its air resistance than that of a small balloon. Like Porter's first plans, Cayley's observations were published in the *Mechanics' Magazine*. See Davy, *Interpretive History of Flight*, 43.

Balance of buoyancy 1,140 lbs, sufficient for five persons with baggage, &c.

The atmospheric resistance against a float of this small size and proportion, is as great as that encountered by the large one.[10]

The estimated cost of an aerial locomotive of the small size, is as follows: —

Cloth for the float, 50 cents per yard	$400
Longitudinal rods	10
Labor in making the float	100
Rudder and its rigging	10
Cost of inflation with zinc hydrogen	500
Cost of saloon, including materials	50
Cost of wires and wheels	100
Engine four-horse power and belt chains	500
Elevator, seats and other items	30
Total cost	$1,700

If inflated with hydrogen produced by a solution of iron, the cost will be $350 less; and if the engine is omitted, the cost will be but $850.

While on the subject of estimates, we will give those of the smallest and cheapest aerial locomotive that it is practicable to construct and navigate, propelling it by a crank.

Length, 120 feet; diameter, 20 feet; contents, 20,000 cubic feet; buoyant power, 1,300 lbs.

Materials.	Weight.	Cost.
Cloth for the float — 400 yards..	200 lbs.	$200
1,200 feet of rods	200	10
Saloon, 25 feet long	200	50
Connecting wires and rudder ...	100	50
Propelling wheels	100	30
Labor in making the float		50
Cost of inflation		110
Total weight and cost,	800 lbs.	$500

Balance of buoyancy — 500 lbs.

To return to the subject of the large locomotive: —It is obvious that no part of the cloth of the float can be subject to a greater pressure than 28 ounces per square foot; for the entire buoyancy of a column of hydrogen one foot square and fifty feet high, can not exceed 53 ounces, and this upward force is equally divided between the pressure of the gas upward against the top and the pressure of the air upward against the bottom of the float.[11] The longitudinal rods are but six feet apart, and it may be readily proved by trial that a strip of light vulcanized cloth one foot wide and six feet long,

being confined at the ends, will sustain at least four times the weight above mentioned. With regard to the weight of the saloon and its contents, one half thereof must be sustained by the cloth, which constitutes the right and left sides of the float. The weight to be thus sustained is about 20,000 pounds, and this weight is sustained by 1600 feet of cloth, — a little more than 12 pounds per foot; yet it is well known that each foot of the cloth will sustain upwards of 100 pounds.

With regard to safety, there appears to be less danger of any accident to the float, than to the hull of even a marine sailing vessel. The float is to be constructed with several apartments, so that if a rent should occur in one part it would not occasion a sudden descent. It appears impossible that the float

[11] The figure 53 is undoubtedly a misprint. That he meant 56 ounces is indicated by his figure of 28 for half that amount. Porter's argument that total buoyant force would be equally divided between the bottom and top of the gas bag was correct if he intended to vent the bag at the vertical midpoint. Nowhere else, however, does he indicate that this was his plan. If he intended to follow the usual system of venting at the bottom, his argument was incorrect, but the difference in stress would have been relatively minor. In his second pamphlet (p. 44) he implies that the whole buoyant force would be exerted on the top.

should ever take fire; and if the saloon should take fire, it can be brought to the ground in three minutes from an ordinary height. Moreover, each passenger will be furnished with an improved parachute by which he can descend from any height without danger. With a parachute eight feet in diameter a man of ordinary weight may descend from any height with less velocity than he would acquire in descending the distance of five feet without it.[12] A gale of wind will not in the least degree affect the float nor the saloon by force or pressure, because the entire apparatus will float with the current; and however strong the wind may be in any direction, the passengers will experience an apparent calm, with the exception of an apparent head wind, produced by the forward motion of the locomotive.[13] A wind that travels 20 miles an hour, is called a fresh sailing breeze; and it is a very severe gale that travels 50 miles per hour; and if, as is expected, the large locomotive is capable of making 100 miles per hour in a calm, it will be able to stem the current of a 50 mile gale, and make 50 miles per hour to windward. Should such a gale blow transversely to the course, it will be only requisite to change the head of the locomotive about 22 degrees to windward, in order to keep on its course; and the distance lost in consequence will be only about 10 miles in 100. Whenever it becomes requisite to stop the machine and come to moorings, it is only required to head the float to the wind, and check the motion of the wheels till the locomotive becomes stationary, when a man may descend in the elevator and secure a small hawser. For this purpose he will be furnished with a large spiral perforator in the form [of] a corkscrew, which he will insert in the earth if there is no permanent object at hand. A large rope is not required to hold the machine, for the severest gale cannot exert a force against it exceeding 50 pounds.[14]

[12] Porter's arithmetic here is correct, if one treats the parachute as a flat plate and uses his own figure for air resistance. In practice, however, the problem is complicated by the need to prevent sideways pitch and "spilling" of air. To attain stability, parachutes must be larger than such a simple calculation would indicate.

[13] At top cruising speed, this apparent head wind would, of course, have been 100 miles per hour. Porter failed throughout to allow for the stresses produced by sudden gusts or changes in wind direction, as well as those created in maneuvering and landing the ship. These factors, which are crucial in modern aircraft design, were not generally recognized until well into the twentieth century.

[14] How Porter arrived at this figure is not altogether clear. It would seem that in addition to other omissions he failed to allow for force exerted upon the car, the rigging, and the propellers.

In case of the approach of a real tornado, the locomotive may either rise above it and let it pass below, or a grapple may be thrown out by which the machine may be brought to safe moorings. In case of a thunderstorm it will not be possible for the float to be ignited by lightning when thus protected by 200 steel wires; but it may sometimes be requisite to throw out one end of a small copper wire to the earth to discharge electricity from the machine.[15]

The attention of the public is drawn to this subject at present with regard, principally, to the facility thereby furnished, of emigration to California; but we have discovered no apparent difficulty in passing over the Atlantic to London or Paris. The machine will carry, in addition to 100 passengers, a sufficient quantity of fuel to last 48 hours, which will be several hours longer than the time required for the passage, under ordinary circumstances. And as it is well known that different and opposite currents prevail at different heights in the air, the machine may run at such elevations as will be most favorable in this respect, and never be compelled to stem a severe head-wind. With regard to a supply of water, it may be readily obtained at any time, though it is proposed to condense the escape steam so as to avoid any waste of water; this may be done by means of two long horizontal pipes exposed to the current of air only. Hydrogen gas is to be constantly supplied by a proper apparatus on board for that purpose.[16]

It may be anticipated that within a few months these aerial machines may be seen soaring in various directions and at different elevations, some apparently among or above the clouds, and others, like swallows, sailing leisurely just above the surface of the earth. The sides of the most lofty and rugged mountains, and the fertile valleys will be alike reconnoitred. Let our gentle readers imagine themselves to be visiting the pleasant and excellent literary establishment on the summit of Mount Holyoke on a sunny morning in the balmy month of June, and gently descending thence towards the verdant plains which border the meandering Connecticut, and then at an elevation of only 8 or 10 feet from the ground

[15] Writing in 1935, Commander Wiley agreed with Porter that the craft was safe from lightning. After the burning of the "Hindenburg" in 1937 there was much discussion over the question. Although it is generally believed that electricity caused the "Hindenburg" fire, the weight of opinion blames a static discharge rather than lightning.

[16] Both here and in his second pamphlet (p. 44), Porter states that the craft would carry equipment for generating hydrogen, yet nowhere in his computations does he allow for the considerable weight of this item.

sailing moderately over the rich fields of broom and grain; and over the flower spangled fields of grass, waiving to the western breeze, and conversing by the way with the merry farmers, as they follow their recreative avocation of hay-making; then ascending with accelerated velocity to the altitude of refreshing temperature and returning to New-York to dine. Or suppose yourselves leisurely cruizing along by the steep and rugged sides of the Rocky Mountains, and laughing at the astonished counte-nance of the harmless grizzly bear, or at the agility of the frightened antelope; and then descending to the extensive prairies to watch the prancing of the wild horses, or the furious rushing of hordes of Buf-faloes. These things are indeed but fancies at present, but in a few months these fancies may become pleasant realities in America, while the proud nations of Europe are staring and wondering at the soaring enterprize of the independent citizens of the United States.

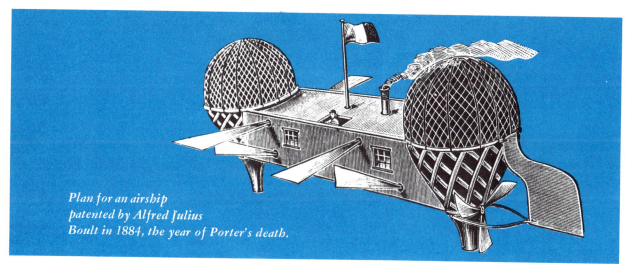

Plan for an airship patented by Alfred Julius Boult in 1884, the year of Porter's death.

AN ÆRIAL STEAMER, OR
FLYING SHIP.

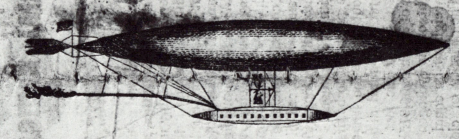

INVENTED BY

RUFUS PORTER,

*Original Editor of the " New-York Mechanic," " Scientific American,"
and " Scientific Mechanic."*

W. GREER, PRINTER, WASHINGTON, D. C. 1850.

EXPLANATION. The general principles of Mr. Porter's plan of aerial navigation, are so plain and simple that they may be readily understood by any person of ordinary *American* intelligence. The most important part, and principal constituent of the apparatus, is an aerial float, made in the form of a *revoloidal spindle* (a long round figure, gradually tapering each way from its centre, and terminating in a point at each end). This is constructed of cotton or linen cloth, coated on one side with India rubber, and the other side with linseed oil paint. This float is supported internally by longitudinal rods of wood and inflated with hydrogen gas. The length of the float (the size proposed to be first constructed) is 700 feet, — about twice the length of a first class steamboat, — and its central diameter 50 feet. It will contain 803,250 cubic feet of hydrogen, the buoyant power of which is 56,915 lbs in atmospheric air; (the weight of the hydrogen being only 4,183 lbs, while the weight of an equal volume of air is 61,098 lbs). The quantity of cloth required in its construction is 7,300 square yards, the weight of which is 7,300 lbs. The weight of 25 longitudinal rods (16,800 feet in length by 1 1-3 inch in diameter) is 4,200 lbs, which added to the weight of the cloth makes 11,500 lbs, or 45,415 lbs less than the buoyant power of the hydrogen.

AN AERIAL STEAMER OR FLYING SHIP

A saloon 150 feet long and 10 feet in diameter, is made of painted cloth with a floor of thin boards; the form of the saloon is similar to that of the float, but with this difference, that the sides of the saloon are vertical, and the top and bottom horizontal. About 80 feet of the central part of the saloon, is furnished with delicate seats for passengers, and with windows in the sides. In the centre of the saloon is an engine room 12 feet by 7, furnished with two light-made steam engines of 10 horse-powers each. The saloon is suspended about 50 feet below the

Porter's plan for an elevated railroad as pictured in the Scientific American *for January 1, 1846.*

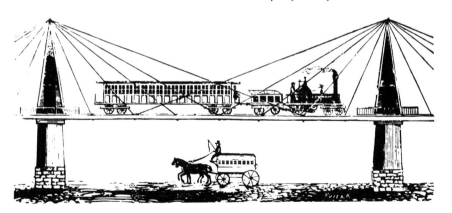

float, being connected thereto by 200 steel rods of the best material, flattened to prevent resistance, and capable of sustaining 1000 lbs each. The floor, sides and top of the saloon are supported in their positions by these rods, the heads of which are attached by screws to the longitudinal rods of the float, at different points. Between the float and saloon are mounted two propelling wheels, 40 feet in diameter and made of light materials. The form of these wheels is similar to that of a marine *steam propeller;* or to an eight-armed windmill wheel: the sails or fans, when in motion, acting obliquely on the air, which by re-action exerts a propulsive force on the wheels, thus propelling the whole machine forward. The wheels are operated by the steam engines by means of belts or endless chains.

To the rear end of the float is connected a rudder 16 feet long, having four leaves four feet wide, two of which are verticle and two horizontal. One edge of each leaf is connected to a central stem, thus forming a ✠, so that the direction of the float may be governed both vertically and horizontally. The rudder is managed by means of four ropes or wires, which extend from the four outward edges of the leaves to the saloon below. The weight of the saloon, together with that of the rudder, wheels, and the supporting rods, is estimated at 3000 lbs; and that of the engines, including water and fuel, at 4000 lbs, thus leaving a balance of buoyancy of 38,415 lbs, —sufficient to carry nearly 200 passengers with their baggage.

SPEED OR VELOCITY

The grand obstacle to aerial navigation, and which has been supposed insurmountable by scientific men in times past, is atmospheric resistance. It is well known that a plane surface, as the end of a cylinder, when moving through the air at a speed of 100 miles per hour, or 146 feet per second, encounters a resistance of at least 32 lbs per square foot. A cylinder 50 feet in diameter, if propelled with this velocity, would encounter a resistance of 62,000 lbs. A spherical balloon of sufficient buoyant power to sustain 45,000 lbs would at this speed, encounter a resistance of at least 100,000 lbs, and would require 26,000 horse-powers to propel it. But it is nevertheless demonstrable that a revoloidal spindle, the length of which is 14 times its diameter, will encounter less than one five thousandth part of the resistance to which a spherical balloon of equal buoyancy would be subjected under equal velocity. The reason of this difference may be explained in few words. It

is a well known fact that the resistance encountered by a body passing through a non-elastic fluid is as the square of its velocity. Therefore if the resistance is 32 lbs per foot when the velocity is 146 feet per second, it would be but 8 lbs with a velocity of 73 feet per second. If the velocity be 36 feet per second the resistance is only 2 lbs. If the velocity be 18 feet, the resistance is ½ lb: —velocity 9 feet, the resistance 2 ounces: and with a velocity of 4½ feet, the resistance is only half an ounce per square foot. Now it will be seen by examining the form of the revoloidal spindle, that the average velocity with which the air is removed, is only about 4½ feet per second, when the forward motion of the spindle is 146 feet per second: consequently the resistance is only half an ounce per square foot; and this resistance being not counter to the forward motion of the float, but in a direction at right angles with the surface thereof, the resistance encountered by the entire forward surface is only equal to a direct resistance of half an ounce per foot on the *area* of the spindle, which amounts to only 60 lbs. This, be it understood, is on the supposition that air is non-elastic, and that it is suddenly put in motion as would be the case if the float was of a wedge shape. But it may be observed that the forward part of the float, near the point, presents but little surface for resistance; and as the surface increases towards the middle, the obliquity thereof decreases, so that the encountered air is gently and gradually put in motion, and as gradually returned to its original position, when the float passes. Moreover, in consequence of the elasticity of the air, and the immense atmospheric pressure which it sustains, it continues to press as forcibly or nearly so, on the rear half of the float as on the forward part, notwithstanding the rapid forward motion of the float. What constitutes atmospheric resistance is a greater pressure of air on the forward part of a moving body, than on the rear or after part; but if the pressure is equal on both, there can be no resistance; for there is no such thing as atmospheric *friction* if the surface is perfectly smooth. But even if the atmospheric resistance was equal to 40 lbs, the 20 horse-powers of steam would be sufficient to overcome it, and continue the speed, even if 45 per cent thereof is allowed for loss of power in the operation of the propelling wheels: for it is readily calculated that if one horse-power will raise 100 lbs, at the rate of 330 feet per minute, or 5½ feet per second, 10 ½ horse-powers will raise 40 lbs 146 feet per second, which is the same as maintaining a speed of 146 feet per

second against a resistance of 40 lbs. It will be seen by the estimate of the buoyant power of the float, however, that a much larger and more powerful engine may be employed, should occasion so require.

MANAGEMENT.

When the float is inflated, the saloon will be freighted with stones or earth in boxes provided for that purpose. When not in use, the machine will be moored at a safe and convenient height, the hawser being secured to some permanent object. A large screw on the principle of a cork-screw to be screwed into the earth by handspike, will be furnished for holding the float on prairie land. One man will be kept constantly on board; and another will be employed as watchman, when the machine is moored. When passengers are to be taken on board, the saloon will be brought to the ground, if the land is clear and the weather calm; otherwise, they will be taken up by an elevator — a horizontal platform, 10 feet long by five wide, and furnished with railings and seats. This elevator is connected to the saloon by four ropes attached to its four corners, and passing over four pullies near the top of the saloon, and thence to a windlass-shaft connected with the steam engine. The elevator when in its place, constitutes a part of the floor of the saloon. When passengers or fuel are received, an equal weight of ballast must be discharged; and vice versa. The amount of ballast will be so restricted that the machine will moderately ascend when freed from its moorings, that it may be the more equally balanced in the air at the height of 500 feet; but in general it will be made to ascend or descend by means of the rudder, and the propulsive force of the wheels. Whenever it is requisite to come to land, to moor the machine, or to land or receive passengers, the rudder will be depressed until the saloon is brought sufficiently near to the earth to send down the elevator. It has been already stated that the saloon is furnished with duplicate engines; but should both of them by any means become impaired at the same time, a grapple may be thrown

out, and will infallibly take to the shrubbery, fences or rocks, and by this the machine may be hauled down. If occasion should so require, however, a part of the hydrogen may be allowed to escape through a valve. In case of running in foggy weather, the height of the machine may be generally ascertained by the barometer; but it will be sometimes requisite to throw out a small line with a lead (or block of wood if over water) for the pur-

AN AERIAL STEAMER

A "Steam-Carriage for Common Roads" shown by Porter in the Scientific American, Oct. 2, 1845.

pose of ascertaining both the elevation of the machine, and the direction and velocity of the wind. (The relative speed of the machine may be known by the revolution of the wheels). The saloon will be furnished with rubber cloth cylinders inflated with air, sufficient to render it a *safety boat* of the best kind, in case of an accidental descent into a lake or ocean.

SAFETY

Several difficulties and dangers have been conjectured by the skeptical opponents of the invention, but which will be noticed in order and shown to be without any rational foundation.

1. It is asserted by some that hydrogen gas is so subtile that cloth can not be so prepared as to retain it. But this conjecture is refuted by the fact that there are now in New Haven several small balloons, made of very thin silk and lightly coated with rubber, but which have been in an inflated state for several months past, without the least apparent diminution of volume or buoyancy. Nevertheless, the machine is to be furnished with apparatus for generating hydrogen in whatever quantity may be required to replenish the float by the way.

2. It has been said that common rubber coated cloth is not strong enough to sustain the weight of the saloon, engine and passengers.

To refute this conjecture, it may be proper to explain briefly the nature and principle of the buoyant power which is to sustain the machine with its freight. Buoyancy does not, as generally supposed consist in a tendency of the hydrogen to ascend and press against the upper side of the float; but what constitutes buoyancy, is a greater atmospheric pressure against the bottom of the float, than upon the top thereof. The weight of air is 527 grains per cubic foot; the weight of a column of air one foot square and 50 feet high, (the diameter of the float) is 3 lbs. 12 ounces. Therefore the atmospheric pressure against the bottom of the float, is greater by 3¾ pounds per square foot than that upon the top thereof: and this would be the true rate of buoyant force were it not for the weight of the hydrogen, which being 4 ounces per 50 cubic feet, reduces the buoyant force to 3½ lbs per foot of the central portion of the float: and this is the greatest force or pressure that is required to be sustained by the cloth. Yet it is readily shown by experiment that the ordinary rubber cloth will sustain more than ten times that amount of pressure, when supported by the longitudinal rods, before mentioned.

3. It is supposed by some that if a rent should by any means occur in any part of the float, the whole apparatus would rapidly descend. But to prevent the possibility of such an event, the float will be furnished with several transverse partitions, so that if a rent should occur in any part, the descent of the machine will be so moderate that the pilot will have time enough to select his ground to land upon. And even if the hydrogen should all escape, the machine could not descend with a greater velocity than sixteen feet per second; — the velocity which a man acquires by descending from a fence or staging four feet high.[1]

4. It has been sometimes averred that no cloth materials would be capable of sustaining the force of a heavy side wind or gale. Those who raise this objection, however, expose their ignorance of the fact, that the aerial machine will float along with the current, and can not be subject to a pressure of half an ounce per square foot by the strongest gale from any direction. Whatever winds may blow, the passengers will experience an apparent calm, except an *apparent head wind* produced by the forward motion of the machine. A head wind will in some measure retard the progress of the machine; but in case of a side wind, it will only be requisite to head the float a few degrees to windward in order to keep its course. With regard to blustering winds or squalls, there can be no such things experienced at the height of half a mile from the earth. The clouds may be always observed to move on their course with a steady motion, however blustering or unsteady the wind may be, near the earth's surface.

5. It has been also conjectured that if the float should take fire, the hydrogen would explode. This supposition also betrays ignorance of the nature of hydrogen, which can no more explode than so much atmospheric air. Should the float be perforated so as to admit the escape of the hydrogen, the escaping current might be ignited, and would burn with a moderate flame; but the fire could not communicate to that within the float.[2] It is impossible, how-

[1] Porter's reasoning here is obscure. Perhaps he counted on the deflated "float" forming a sort of parachute. No doubt he was familiar with the experiments of the aeronaut John Wise, who had shown in 1838 that a burst balloon would, under the right circumstances, descend slowly. The rigid frame of Porter's airship would have prevented this, however. See Wise, *A System of Aeronautics*, 60, 190–198.

[2] Porter assumed that the hydrogen within the float could be kept pure and unmixed with oxygen. Experience has shown that where a fabric skin is used, this is unlikely to be the case.

ever, that fire should be communicated to the float or its contents. Sparks from the furnace can never come in contact with the float when in motion; and if they should, they could never ignite the smooth rubber coating of the cloth. The saloon will be made fire-proof by a saline saturation of the cloth and the floor. A spark of lightning cannot perforate the rubber cloth, nor come in contact therewith, while so many steel rods are connected thereto.

The principles and construction of this invention have been explained to several thousands of persons, most of whom have been apparently convinced of the practicability of its successful operation; and among them several of the most scientific men in the United States. Every obstacle and difficulty that could be imagined, have been brought up by those who were strongly opposed to its success; these have been duly considered, discussed and obviated. The only circumstance which has hitherto prevented this invention from successful operation, has been the want of the requisite funds: for unfortunately, capitalists are generally either shamefully ignorant of scientific principles, or are such slaves to pride and popularity as to be ashamed to patronize a new invention; or are so enviously adverse to the fortunes of inventors as to refuse to aid, unless on such con-

ditions as to grasp the invention and ruin its author. But this important invention is destined to succeed eventually, and constitute the principal and general instrument of transportation of merchandise, as well as mails and passengers throughout the world.

The following brief extracts from different newspapers, will suffice to show that Mr. Porter's experiments on a small scale, have been successful.

A large number of literary and scientific gentlemen, among whom were Professor Ewbank, Professors from the N.Y. University and Columbia College and representatives from most of the daily and Sunday papers, attended yesterday a second exhibition of the Aerial Steamer. It is now fairly before the public, and as the model does fly, there is little doubt of the invention being completely successful. — *N.Y. Sun.*

The Ariel Steamer Model was again tried at the Merchant's Exchange yesterday afternoon, and with brilliant success. It described the circle of the rotunda eleven times in succession, following its rudder like a thing instinct with life. With its description of each circle, burst after burst of applause arose from the excited throng, and followed it throughout its journey. At the close of the performance, three loud cheers were given for the steamer, and the auditors quitted the rotunda with every manifestation of pleasure and delight. — *N.Y. True Sun.*

The Model Aerial Steamer was exhibited again in the Merchant's Exchange yesterday, and satisfied some of its greatest opponents that it could navigate the air. — *N.Y. Sun.*

Mr. Porter's "flying machine" did all that it promised on Wednesday evening. It rose above the audience, and went round the hall, exactly as he said it would, and the spectators gave three cheers for the successful experiment. — *Boston Bee.*

The flying machine did fly last evening, though rather low. At the second and third attempts, the apparatus went round the hall, just over the heads of the auditory, very satisfactorily, and elicited three hearty cheers from the spectators. Mr. Porter may be considered as having fairly demonstrated the theory of aerial navigation; but it is only in the open air that the practicability of the theory can be demonstrated. — *Boston Mail.*

Porter's design for a "Bullet Engine," or revolving rifle, as presented in the August 6, 1846, issue of the **Scientific American.**

INDEX

NUMBER *1,863*

of an edition limited to two thousand copies. *A Yankee Inventor's Flying Ship* was printed by Lund Press of Minneapolis. The text is set in 10-point Linotype Janson and printed on stock of 70-pound Nekoosa Offset with vellum finish.